Edexcel P
Confl
Anthology

The Ultimate Audio Revision Guide

By Emily Bird and Jeff Thomas

How does anger drive the narrators of 'A Poison Tree and 'The Class Game'?

Introduction

- In *A Poison Tree*, the narrator is driven to dark thoughts and deeds by their anger while in *The Class Game*, the narrator's anger fuels a passionate defence of their life and culture.

Context

- Blake had a great interest in social reform and used his poetry to try and teach people that communication is the key to dealing with feelings of anger.
- Casey does just as Blake advised and expresses her anger at being made to feel inadequate because of her working class roots. In doing so, her anger converts to defiance and then to a bold celebration of her heritage.

Language

- Blake uses an extended metaphor of the apple tree to represent the narrator's anger as something that is growing.
- Casey uses phonetic spellings and dialect words, such as '**corpy**' to add to the angry (yet proud) tone of the poem.

Form

- Both poems use rhyming couplets. Blake uses them consistently throughout the entire poem, giving it a sing-song quality; this suggests the narrator's anger is immature and childish. Casey's use of rhyming couplets is consistent but less rigid; this creates strength in her poem and underscores the feelings of anger and pride.

Structure

- Both poems end with a note of triumph. Blake's narrator feels victorious when he sees his '**foe outstretch'd**' while Casey's narrator firmly states that she is '**proud of the class**' that she's from.
- Although both poems end with a sense of victory, readers are likely to feel revulsion at the narrator of *A Poison Tree,* as he is behaving and thinking in an immoral way, whereas readers will empathise with the narrator in Casey's poem, as she has used it to express her anger in a way that explains her grievances and also celebrates her class.

How do the poems 'The Destruction of Sennacherib' and 'Poppies' explore the effects of war?

troduction

Both poems show that war brings suffering and pain to family members of the men involved in the conflict. In Byron's poem the '**widows**' grieve for their lost husbands and sons, while in *Poppies*, the mother grieves over losing her son to adulthood and possibly death.

ntext

Byron alludes to Biblical accounts of Sennacherib's attack on Jerusalem and his focus is on the Assyrians as a nation. He shows that the defeat of Sennacherib's army brings about collective grief and forces the war widows to question their faith, while Weir's poem focuses on the sense of loss felt by one mother, giving it a more intimate feel.

nguage

Byron uses the temporal language of '**sunset**' and then '**morrow**' to make it clear that the Assyrian army is defeated overnight, while Weir's use of temporal language brings ambiguity to her poem. Phrases like '**Before you left**' and '**After you'd gone**', could refer to the son leaving for school, joining the army, or hinting that the son is dead. While the Assyrian widows feel the effects of war in a definite way, the uncertainty of life is what's affecting the mother in *Poppies*.

rm

The regular quatrains and the use of rhyming couplets give Byron's poem a sense of order and seems to suggest that justice has prevailed in the battle, while the free verse of Weir's poem suits the fact that it is more ambiguous, the reader can never be sure whether the son is parted from his mother in some way, or actually killed in action.

ructure

Both poems end with references to sound. In Byron's poem, the widows '**wail**' as they react to the outcome of the battle, while in *Poppies*, the mother strains to hear her son's '**playground' voice**'. This shows that in the face of an ambiguous situation the mother feels anxiety rather than the raw grief felt by the Assyrians.

Explore how the theme of regret features in 'The Prelude' and 'The Man He Killed'.

Introduction

- Both narrators regret aspects of their past, however, the character in *The Prelude* can see that his loss of innocence is an essential part of growing up, whereas the speaker in *The Man He Killed* intimates that his sorry situation could have been avoided.

Context

- Wordsworth believed that significant memories surfaced in the consciousness, calling them 'spots of time'. *The Prelude* describes an instance that features feelings of regret.
- Hardy had a particular interest in the Napoleonic Wars and interviewed veterans of that conflict. It's likely these conversations informed him that regret was a key feeling expressed by the soldiers he spoke to.

Language

- Both narrators struggle to express their regret. Wordsworth uses the extended metaphor of the '**peak, black and huge**' to convey that his regret is just one strand of a much larger experience. The narrator in Hardy's poem describes war as '**quaint and curious**', this use of litotes shows that words fail him as he tries to communicate his regret.

Form

- The unrhymed lines and iambic pentameter mean that *The Prelude* sounds naturalistic, and this suits the content, as the poet is sharing a private moment of regret and doesn't want his thoughts overshadowed by elaborate verse.
- The sophisticated form of Hardy's poem elevates the straightforward language, so that the man is able to communicate his regret in a way that is profound, rather than it just being an anecdote.

Structure

- Wordsworth introduces a volta on line 21 to mark the change from an exciting experience to one the narrator will come to regret. Whereas the sense of regret is present right from the start of Hardy's poem.

Explore how loss is central to the poems 'The Man He Killed' and 'What Were They Like?'.

ıtroduction

- In Hardy's poem the narrator has personally lost faith in himself and humanity, while in Levertov's poem an entire nation and its culture has been lost.

ɔntext

- Hardy's poem was written in 1902, the year the Boer Wars ended, and was in response to all the loss suffered during these conflicts.
- Levertov uses her poem to speculate on the results of America's bombing campaigns used during the Vietnam War, showing that a whole nation could be lost.

ınguage

- In Hardy's poem, line 9 ends with a <u>dash</u> in order to create a pause in the poem, showing the narrator is lost for words; this betrays deeper feeling of loss resulting from his participation in conflict.
- In Levertov's poem, line 15 tells the reader that '**there were no more buds**', this <u>metaphor</u> refers to a loss of new life in general and the loss of children in particular.

ɔrm

- Both forms encourage readers to reflect on the theme of loss. The <u>monologue</u> of Hardy's poem allows his narrator to express his personal sense of loss, while the <u>question and answer form</u> of Levertov's poem encourages readers to consider loss in a wider sense, and think about how it would be to lose an entire nation and their culture.

ːructure

- In *The Man He Killed* the <u>enjambment</u> from line 12 into 13 links stanzas three and four. This shows that as the man reflects on his past he can no longer contain his feelings, the overflowing lines symbolize his overwhelming sense of loss.
- In *What Were They Like?* the poem <u>ends with the statement</u> '**It is silent now**'; after all the hesitant answers, this is the one definite statement the second speaker can make. It leaves the reader with a lasting impression of bleakness and loss.

<u>Investigate how family is central to the poems 'Cousin Kate' and 'Catrin'.</u>

Introduction

- In *Cousin Kate*, the narrator is hurt by a family member but is left with a child that brings her joy; in *Catrin* the mother has a daughter who brings her both hurt and joy.

Context

- In *Cousin Kate*, Rossetti criticizes Victorian double standards, whereby women would be left ruined by an affair, while men were untouched. Rossetti goes on to show that although the narrator's son is proof of her '**shame**', she also loves him fiercely, showing that bonds of family love transcend social rules.
- *Catrin*, written over a hundred years later, echoes the notion that the bond between mother and child is strong but also filled with conflicting emotions.

Language

- Both poems show that being a mother brings conflicting emotions. Rossetti <u>juxtaposes</u> the feelings of '**shame**' and '**pride**' on line 45 to illustrate the conflict.
- In *Catrin*, the '**Red rope of love**' is a <u>metaphor</u> for the physica and emotional ties between a mother and child. Clarke picks up this image later in the poem saying the rope is '**Tightening about my life**' to show that the love a mother has for her child can be so fierce it's almost suffocating.

Form

- *Cousin Kate* is a <u>ballad</u>; a form often used to narrate cautionary tales. Here the poet warns against the double standards Victorian society had for women.
- *Catrin* is written in <u>free verse</u> which suits the fact that the poem is exploring private, personal events.

Structure

- In *Cousin Kate*, the narrator's <u>final wish</u> is that her son will '**wear his coronet**', while in *Catrin*, the mother wishes that she could protect her daughter from harm.
- Both of these scenarios are unlikely. It's improbable that the lord will give his title to an illegitimate child and it is impossible to protect children from all risks.

How is racism addressed in the poems 'Half-caste' and 'No Problem'?

ntroduction

- Both poems show that despite great advances in equality, racism still exists in modern UK culture.

ontext

- The title *Half-caste* brings to mind other racist terms such as mulatto and quadroon, which were used to describe people in terms of how much black ancestry they had. These labels were used to identify people as being racially 'un-pure', leaving them open to exploitation and prejudice.
- Zephaniah suggests that British culture can accept black people becoming elite athletes, but it doesn't allow them to rise in other areas such as academia.

anguage

- Both poems use phonetic spelling. Agard mixes phonetic spelling with Standard English, and in this way, uses the language itself to show that cultures in combination can be used as a medium for greatness and beauty.
- Zephaniah's phonetic spelling communicates a Caribbean accent, and this gives the reader a clear indication of the narrator's heritage, showing they speak from experience.

orm

- *Half-caste* is in free verse, which reflects the fact that it is trying to free readers from prejudiced thoughts.
- In Zephaniah's poem, stanza one envelopes four quatrains within it. This strict form could reflect the way black people are put into strict stereotyped roles such as athletes.

tructure

- *Half-caste* has a volta at the start of line 47, where the narrator turns the concept of being a half-caste on to his audience. If you don't look '**wid de whole of yu eye**', you are only receiving half the information, making you the 'half-caste'.
- In *No Problem*, '**I am not de problem**' is repeated four times within the first stanza. This reinforces the idea that it's society that's imposing racist values on black people, and this is what's causing the problem.

How do the poems 'Exposure' and 'Half-caste' explore the idea of control?

Introduction

- In *Exposure*, the men are in a situation beyond their control. They have no jurisdiction over the governments that are at war, and even less control over the freezing weather, the mos deadly of enemies. In *Half-caste*, the narrator shows that modern British society still tries to control black people.

Context

- Owen explores the themes of patriotism and faith in the poen and suggests that these are what motivate men to submit to being controlled and sent to their deaths.
- The term half-caste was commonly used to describe people who had parents from different cultural backgrounds. It is a racist term as it belittles people making them sound incomplete and therefore easily controllable.

Language

- In *Exposure*, Owen personifies the weather with phrases like '**pale flakes... come feeling for our faces**' in order to show that it is a deadly enemy that controls and kills the men.
- Agard also uses weather imagery and the metaphor '**dem clouds... don't want de sun pass**' is used to show that black people face barriers and control.

Form

- *Exposure* has a very regular, controlled form that reflects the lack of choice the soldiers have as they wait to die.
- *Half-caste* is written in free verse, as if the poem itself has been liberated from any form of control.

Structure

- In *Exposure*, each stanza ends with a half line. In stanzas one, three, four and eight, the line '**But nothing happens**' is repeated, and this refrain emphasizes the crushing feeling of despair and paralysis that all the soldiers feel as they are controlled by their government, the enemy and the weather.
- *Half-caste* also employs a refrain, the phrase '**explain yuself**' is repeated four times throughout the poem in order to challenge those who seek to control the lives of the black population.

Compare the portrayal of the soldiers in 'The Charge of the Light Brigade' and 'The Destruction of Sennacherib'.

ntroduction

- In Tennyson's poem the British soldiers are portrayed as brave and loyal, while in Byron's poem, the Assyrian soldiers are portrayed as merciless and overly proud.

ontext

- There is no definitive answer as to why the '**six hundred**' were sent on their suicide mission, however it's likely to be a combination of miscommunication and mismanagement.
- At the time Byron's poem was written, Britain had been involved in the Napoleonic Wars for over a decade, it's arguable that by portraying the defeat of the Assyrian army, Byron was giving hope to the British.

anguage

- In Tennyson's poem '**Death**' is personified, to show the British soldiers have an impossible task ahead of them, thus enhancing their bravery when they carry out their orders.
- Byron uses the simile '**like a wolf**' to describe the Assyrians, making them sound fierce; it also dehumanises them and brings them down to the level of beasts.

orm

- In Tennyson's poem, the irregular form portrays the movement of the soldiers during the charge, as they try to stay in a formation, but are forced apart by enemy fire.
- In Byron's poem, the meter produces a very buoyant rhythm, which could reflect the initial confidence the Assyrians feel as they prepare to attack.

tructure

- Each stanza ends with a reference to the '**six hundred**'. This gives the reader both the whole story and has an emotive effect, showing that the structure is carefully crafted. This strong structure could represent the strength of the soldiers' loyalty.
- The volta appears half way through stanza two, before this, the Assyrian army are portrayed as powerful and proud, afterwards they are shown to be no match for God.

How do the poems 'Catrin' and 'Belfast Confetti' explore feelings of tension?

Introduction

- *Catrin* explores the feelings of tension generated by the deep bond of love between a mother and child, while *Belfast Confetti* looks at political tension.

Context

- Clarke has a daughter called Catrin, so the reader could assume that this poem is autobiographical; it explores the feelings of love and tension from a personal perspective.
- Ireland endured a conflict called The Troubles, which ran from 1968 until 1998. Bombings were a feature of the tensions seen during The Troubles.

Language

- *Catrin* has a lexis of conflict, with words such as '**struggle**' and '**confrontation**' showing tension exists in the relationship.
- At the end *Belfast Confetti*, the narrator says he suffers the rap fire of '**question marks**', this metaphor shows that everyone in the area is a suspect and that feelings of fear, suspicion and tension are running high.

Form

- In *Catrin*, the gap in between the two stanzas represents two different time periods, but could also symbolise that there is a distance between the mother and daughter due to tensions ir the relationship.
- The fragmented form of *Belfast Confetti* creates cul-de-sacs o the page and could symbolise the dead ends of the failed peace talks that went on during this era of Irish history.

Structure

- Clarke juxtaposes victory and defeat in the line '**Neither won nor lost**' to show there's tension between feelings of love and identity within a parent/child bond.
- In *Belfast Confetti*, the extra-long lines are combined with enjambment, the tension here means that the reader is constantly having to move their eyes back and forth across and down the page, this creates a sense of disorientation and gives the reader a sense of what it feels like to be the narrator, caught in the blast.

How do 'War Photographer' and 'A Poison Tree' explore the difference between right and wrong?

ntroduction

- In *War Photographer*, the narrator tries to document conflict in good faith, but an underlying sense of unease haunts them.
- In *A Poison Tree*, the narrator seems to understand the difference between right and wrong, and yet he is '**glad**' when his foe is harmed.

ontext

- Some people would say that war photographers make their money by exploiting the suffering of others, while the counter argument is that the public needs the truth.
- In *A Poison Tree*, Blake explores the fact that humans know the difference between right and wrong, and yet they often choose to indulge their '**fears**'.

anguage

- The photographer says that if an image is troubling, viewers tell themselves that just beyond the frame '**people eat, sleep and love normally**'. Viewers apply their own ideas and this blurs the lines between right and wrong.
- In Blake's poem, the image of the apple is an allusion to the forbidden fruit eaten by Adam and Eve, and enhances the theme of right and wrong.

orm

- *War Photographer* does not follow a set form, possibly reflecting the idea that life is '**arbitrary**'.
- *A Poison Tree* has a regular form, which is at odds with the irregular content.

tructure

- The structure of War Photographer weaves backwards and forwards throughout, and the reader suspects that the '**blood stain on a wall**' is connected to the girl and baby. This highlights the crux of the matter, was it right or wrong to take and publish the photograph bearing in mind what happened next.
- In Blake's poem, 14 out of 16 lines are end-stopped, giving the poem a measured quality with the impression that the story is being recounted in a precise way so that the moral can be easily perceived.

What do the poems 'Belfast Confetti' and 'The Prelude' have to say about the nature of fear?

Introduction

- In both poems, fear is generated as a result of a significant moment in time. In *Belfast Confetti* it is the bomb blast and in *The Prelude* it is the witnessing of the black peak.

Context

- Throughout history, Ireland has suffered from external invasions and internal conflicts, for example Henry VIII sought to rule Ireland during Tudor Times. As a result, fear of conflict persists.
- Wordsworth's work falls into the genre of Romanticism, a movement that looked to explore individual experiences and emotions, including feelings of dread and fear.

Language

- Carson uses the metaphor '**raining exclamation marks**' to illustrate the highly emotional shouts of fear and pain that are all around him directly after the bomb blast.
- Wordsworth uses the simile '**like a living thing**' to shows that he knows this peak isn't a real threat itself, but that he has come to understand that the world does have threats.

Form

- In *Belfast Confetti*, the lines are physically too long to fit into the width of a standard size page and they are forced onto the line below. This creates a labyrinth look to the poem, and reflects the sense of loss and fear the narrator feels.
- Wordsworth understood that human nature is complicated, so it's fitting that he chose the epic form for The Prelude.

Structure

- *Belfast Confetti* begins in medias res, as the bomb has just gone off and the '**riot squad**' are taking action. This structuring reflects the fact that the narrator is caught in the middle of a frightening situation.
- Despite all the beauty and excitement felt earlier in *The Prelude*, it ends on a sombre note. This shows that Wordsworth wanted his reader to appreciate that the sense of fear lingered long after the experience of rowing on the lake was over.

What do the poems 'The Class Game' and 'Cousin Kate' have to say about social class?

ntroduction

- In both poems the narrators are working class, and suffer because of their social status.

ontext

- Determining class can be quite complex, but factors such as your occupation, level of education and choice of leisure activities all contribute to shaping your class identity.
- *Cousin Kate* illustrates how working class Victorian women were vulnerable and could be manipulated by others.

anguage

- In *The Class Game* the line '**Don't I crook me little finger when I drink me tea**' is significant. While class may determine the way tea is made or drunk, it has universal appeal. Other drinks may have class connotations, tea does not. Tea transcends class and demonstrates that there are aspects of British society that run deeper than class. The logical conclusion to this argument is that people should not let class divide them because essentially we are all equal.
- In Rossetti's poem, Kate is seen at her '**father's gate**', here the gate symbolises that Kate is protected by another man, whereas the narrator doesn't mention any family. This could explain why the lord is able to cast the narrator aside but marries Kate; even though both girls are of low social status.

'orm

- The speaker in Casey's poem pours out their defence of being working class, and this gathers pace. The outpouring of emotion and arguments is reflected in the fact that the poem is <u>one long stanza, with no breaks</u>.
- The <u>strong rhyme scheme</u> in *Cousin Kate* enhances the sound of the poem when it is performed aloud.

tructure

- The <u>question and answer structure</u> brings a didactic tone and aims to educate the reader that being working class does not make you inferior to anyone else.
- In *Cousin Kate*, the narrator <u>repeats</u> the idea that she is a '**thing**'. The lord was able to treat her like a possession due to her low social status and resulting lack of power.

What role does memory play in the poems 'Poppies' and 'The Charge of the Light Brigade'?

Introduction

- In *Poppies*, the mother conjures memories of her son to soothe her troubled mind. *The Charge of the Light Brigade* honours the soldiers that fought and died in the infamous battle, so that their deeds will never be forgotten.

Context

- Since time began, mothers have had to say goodbye to their sons when they leave to go to war, and *Poppies* explores this situation.
- The Light Brigade made their fateful charge during the Battle of Balaclava.

Language

- Poppies uses tactile imagery with words such as '**smoothed**' and '**graze**', to reflect the fact that the mother is recalling moments when she was physically close to her son.
- Tennyson's poem uses rhetorical questions such as '**When can their glory fade?**' in order to challenge the reader and ensure that they make a conscious effort never to forget this brave, yet senseless event.

Form

- The free verse of *Poppies* reflects the way memories occur in the mind, sometimes following a chain of events, sometimes jumping to a new memory.
- The irregular form of Tennyson's poem reflects the irregular orders that the soldiers faithfully followed in order to highlight the bravery that should never be forgotten.

Structure

- The memories that the mother brings to mind in Weir's poem seem disordered rather than chronological, this is essential in maintaining the ambiguity in the poem, so that the reader can never be sure if the son is dead or just elsewhere.
- Whereas the events in Tennyson's poem are in chronological order. This structuring allows the reader to follow the soldiers as they make their brave attack and then try and return, thus emphasizing why their story should always be remembered.

What role does hope play in the poems 'No Problem' and 'Exposure'.

ıtroduction

In *No Problem*, the narrator communicates a hopeful tone. Despite suffering from '**racist stunts**' he has '**no chips**' on his shoulders and wants to move forward to a society that is fair. In *Exposure*, the narrator and his fellow soldiers are without hope, facing enemy fire and freezing conditions.

›ntext

After WW2 many people emigrated from the Caribbean to Britain. On arrival, they faced racism, for example, boarding houses would openly display signs saying 'No Blacks'.
The Western Front in World War I was characterised by trench warfare, where the opposing sides, 'dug in' and waged their conflict across the no-man's land in between.

ınguage

The narrator of *No Problem* creates an open, hopeful tone. He greets people with a '**smile**' and would '**teach**' them about other cultures if they allowed him to; despite facing insidious racism, he is not bitter and the reader can believe him when he says '**I have no chips on me shoulders**'.

- <u>Assonance</u> appears with the line '**Shutters and doors, all closed: on us the doors are closed-**'. Here the repeated vowel sounds stretch out the pace and slow it down, creating a sense of hopelessness.

›rm

- In *No Problem* stanza 2 is less restricted in form than stanza 1 and reflects the message of the poem, which is to say that there is hope for the future and one day we will '**get it right**'.
- In *Exposure* every stanza has four full lines, followed by a half line, so nothing different happens to the stanzas throughout the poem, creating a sense of stagnation and hopelessness.

tructure

- *No Problem* uses <u>enjambment</u> numerous times so the poem flows, suggesting that the narrator will keep broadcasting his message until society has rid itself of racism.
- The majority of the lines in *Exposure* are <u>end-stopped</u>. This slow pace mirrors the sense of torpor and hopelessness that the soldiers feel.

How is suffering depicted in 'What Were They Like?' and 'War Photographer'?

Introduction

- Both poems depict suffering caused by war; Levertov shows an entire nation suffering, while Satyamurti focuses on the suffering of an individual girl who becomes a casualty.

Context

- American bombing raids against Vietnam used technology such as cluster bombs and napalm, both of which caused horrific suffering to casualties.
- No specific conflict is named in *War Photographer,* making it universal. This allows the poem to comment that innocent civilians continue to suffer as a result of war.

Language

- Levertov uses alliteration in the phrase '**bitter to the burned mouth**' in order to highlight the suffering of the Vietnamese.
- In *War Photographer*, the use of the phrase '**first bomb of the morning**' is chilling in tone as it implies that there will be more afterwards and emphasizes that the girl and the baby have to suffer the constant threat of being injured or killed.

Form

- *What Were They Like?* is formed of two stanzas. Stanza one is a list of questions and stanza two is made up of the corresponding answers. This means that the poem can be read straight through, or it can be read by alternating between the questions and their answers.
- The free verse of *War Photographer* reflects the fact they are sharing personal memories.

Structure

- In *What Were They Like?* the second speaker speculates that fathers would have spent their time telling '**old tales**' to their sons. This peaceful scene is juxtaposed with the image that there was '**time only to scream**' after the bombs started to fall, showing the suffering of the Vietnamese.
- In *War Photographer*, the pair of girls in stanza two are juxtaposed with the two children in stanza three, in order to highlight the fact that while some people are carefree, others are enduring suffering.

How to compare two unseen poems

an your answer

Making a table of similarities and differences could help to plan your answer.

omparison is key

Ensure that you make constant comparisons throughout your work rather than discussing first one poem and then the other.

- Each point you make should refer to both poems.

Use comparative connectives such as 'whereas', 'likewise' and 'on the other hand' to draw your points together.

ompare the surface story

- Identify the surface story in your second poem and then see how this relates to the first poem. This will help to get you started.

ompare the language

- Look for language techniques and consider which poem is more effective at conveying its message through such techniques.
- Compare the narrators used in the poems, then state which narrator sounds more sympathetic or believable.
- Compare any autobiographical elements, state whether you think direct experience adds value to the unseen poems?
- Consider the intended audience of both poems, and state which is more successful at communicating its point to its chosen audience.
- Consider the purpose of both poems and state which one is better at achieving its purpose.

ompare the titles

- Consider the titles and see which is better at conveying layers of meaning.
- Maybe one title is too literal, or too obscure to be truly effective, whilst the other perfectly sums up the poem.

ompare patterns in the form

- If one poem has a regular form and the other is irregular, what effect does this have on the reader?
- Do both poems break patterns to create effects? If so, which poem does this more effectively?

ompare the structures

- Do the poems employ similar use of stanzas? Which poem is better at using its stanzas to build up its message?
- Do both poems use a volta? Were either of the turning points a surprise? If so, what effect does this have on the reader?
- Are there any similarities or differences in the way the poems are laid out? Do you prefer one structure to another?
- Does one poem use more enjambment or end-stopped lines than the other? Which poem is more effective in its use of these techniques?
- Do both poems use repetition? If so, which poem does this more effectively?
- Compare the opening and closing images in the poems and discuss which you find more compelling.

ind your evidence

- Ensure that you use quotations and refer directly to the poems to prove your points.
- You may want to use a Point, Evidence, Explain, Link structure.
- As an alternative, you may want to blend short quotes into your writing.

Suggested poems for use when preparing for the unseen poetry questions.

The following is a list of suggested poems that would be suitable for a GCSE pu to use when revising for the unseen poetry question. Try pairing them and findi similarities and differences.

A Martian Sends a Postcard Home by Craig Raine
Afternoons by Philip Larkin
Amen by Christina Rossetti
An Advancement of Learning by Seamus Heaney
Ballad of the Bread Man by Charles Causley
Bedtime Story by George Macbeth
Blackberrying by Sylvia Plath
Churning Day by Seamus Heaney
First Love by John Clare
I *Shall Return* by Claude McKay
La Belle Dame Sans Merci by John Keats
Long Distance by Tony Harrison
Mirror by Sylvia Plath
My Grandmother by Elizabeth Jennings
Once Upon a Time by Gabriel Okara
Porphyria's Lover by Robert Browning
Roe-Deer by Ted Hughes
Sonnet 18 by William Shakespeare
Sonnet 116 by William Shakespeare
The Flea by John Donne
The Road Not Taken by Robert Frost
The Sick Equation by Brian Pattern
To Autumn by John Keats
To His Coy Mistress by Andrew Marvell

The following is a list of suggested poems in pairs that would again be suitable for a GCSE pupil to use when revising for the unseen poetry comparison question.

Compare the theme of place in *Hard Water* by Jean Sprackland and *A Vision* by Simon Armitage.

Compare the presentation of love in *Hour* by Carol Ann Duffy and *Nettles* by Vernon Scanell.

Compare the narrators in *Medusa* by Carol Ann Duffy and *The River God* by Stevie Smith.

Compare how the poets explore the idea of allies and enemies in *The Right Word* by Imtiaz Dharker and *The Yellow Palm* by Robert Minhinnick.